THE BEST
DOGS
EVER

PUGS
ARE THE
BEST!

Elaine Landau

LERNER PUBLICATIONS COMPANY · MINNEAPOLIS

For David Loertscher

Lerner Publications Company
A division of Lerner Publishing Group, Inc.
241 First Avenue North
Minneapolis, MN 55401 U.S.A.

Website address: www.lernerbooks.com

Library of Congress Cataloging-in-Publication Data

Landau, Elaine.
    Pugs are the best! / by Elaine Landau.
    p.   cm. — (The best dogs ever)
    Includes index.
    ISBN 978-0-7613-5058-3 (lib. bdg. : alk. paper)
    1. Pug—Juvenile literature. I. Title.
  SF429.P9L36 2011
  636.76—dc22   2009016420

Manufactured in the United States of America
1 — BP — 7/15/10

TABLE OF CONTENTS

CHAPTER ONE

HUG A PUG

Would you like a dog that could make you smile? How about a flat-faced pooch with a curly tail? Is a playful and loving pup right up your alley?

If you said yes to the above, then you might like a pug!

Good Things Come in Small Packages

Pugs are sturdy dogs with small but solid bodies. They stand between 12 and 14 inches (30 and 36 centimeters) high. They weigh up to 18 pounds (8 kilograms). That's about the weight of two house cats.

Pugs aren't much larger than a cat!

Pugs have wrinkly muzzles, round heads, and big eyes. Their coats are short, smooth, and soft. Pugs' coats come in either black or fawn. Some fawn pugs' coats have hints of apricot or silver.

Some pugs are all one color—like this one. Others—like the one on the opposite page—might have markings on their muzzles or elsewhere on their fur.

GREAT NAMES FOR A GREAT PET

Think your pug is the perfect pet? Then give it a name both you and your dog can be proud of. See if any of these fit your charming pooch.

Snuggles   Gizmo   PICKLE   Lola

Gordie

SPIKE   WRINKLES   Pigtail

WHOOPIE   Jester

Quite a Pooch

Pugs are tons of fun. These pooches are friendly and outgoing. They also look great in dog clothes! Some say a pug is really a clown in a dog's body.

SAME DOG, DIFFERENT NAMES

Pugs live in many places around the world. But not everyone calls them pugs. In China, they are called foo dogs. In Tibet, they are known as hand dogs. In France, people call them carlins.

Pugs welcome visitors and tend to play well with other pets. But they are really happiest around their special humans. Many owners just want to hug their pugs. They think that pugs are the best.

CHAPTER TWO

FROM THEN TO NOW

Pugs have a proud history. Dogs similar to pugs once lived in ancient China. Chinese emperors (powerful rulers) kept these flat-faced dogs as pets. The dogs ate the finest food and slept on silk pillows.

By the tenth century, large numbers of these dogs were being bred in Chinese palaces. The longer-haired dogs became the Pekingese breed. The dogs with shorter coats became pugs.

This statue was made in China more than two thousand years ago. It shows a pug.

A Traveling Dog

During the 1600s and 1700s, traders brought pugs to Europe. Royal people in many countries there adored these pint-sized pooches. So did the rich upper classes. Famous artists painted pugs. Writers wrote about them.

This Russian princess has a pug. The portrait was painted in the 1750s.

FIT FOR A QUEEN

Queen Victoria (left) of the United Kingdom loved little dogs. Pugs were among her favorites. The queen had five pugs! She also bred these dogs.

The love of pugs continued through the years. In the 1940s, the Duke and Duchess of Windsor—a royal couple who lived in France—had about eleven pugs at different times. The couple traveled with their dogs. The dogs' personal chef traveled with them too. He served the pugs their meals on sterling silver plates.

The Duke and Duchess of Windsor brought their pugs to California in 1959.

Loved Everywhere

Pugs were a hit when they were brought to the United States as well. This was especially true during the 1950s and 1960s. These canine cuties appeared in many dog shows then.

AND THE WINNER IS . . .

The year 1981 was wonderful for pugs. That year, a pug won Best in Show at the Westminster Kennel Club Dog Show. The winner was a four-year-old beauty named Dhandy's Favorite Woodchuck (right, with his handler, Bobby Barlow). His owner called him Chucky. It was the first and only time a pug ever won top honors at Westminster.

Pugs are still well liked in modern times. People find them hard to resist. In fact, pugs are among the United States' twenty most popular dog breeds.

Toy Dogs

The American Kennel Club (AKC) groups dogs by breed. Some of the AKC's groups are the sporting group, the herding group, and the hound group. Pugs are in the toy group.

Afghan hounds are in the hound group.

This German shepherd is in the herding group.

Springer spaniels, like this one, are in the sporting group.

Chihuahuas are in the toy group— just like pugs!

All dogs in the toy group are small. You may have stuffed animals bigger than these pooches. Many toy dogs make great pets. The pug is one of these!

15

CHAPTER THREE

IS A PUG RIGHT FOR YOU?

Who wouldn't want a pug? It's hard to find a cuter or a sweeter dog. And pugs are as loyal as a dog can be.

So isn't a pug the perfect pet for everyone? Well, not quite. No dog is right for everyone. Read on to see if a pug is right for you.

Things Are Getting Hairy

Pugs have sleek, shiny coats. These dogs don't need a lot of grooming. This is a big plus. Yet pugs do shed a lot. If you get a pug, you'll find pug hair all over your clothes and house. Be ready for fur in the air and everywhere.

A Dog That Needs Company

Pugs were bred to be with people. They hate being alone. Do you have after-school activities on most days? Will someone be at home with your pug when you're not? If your pet must be by itself most of the day, pick another pooch. A lonely, bored pug is an unhappy dog.

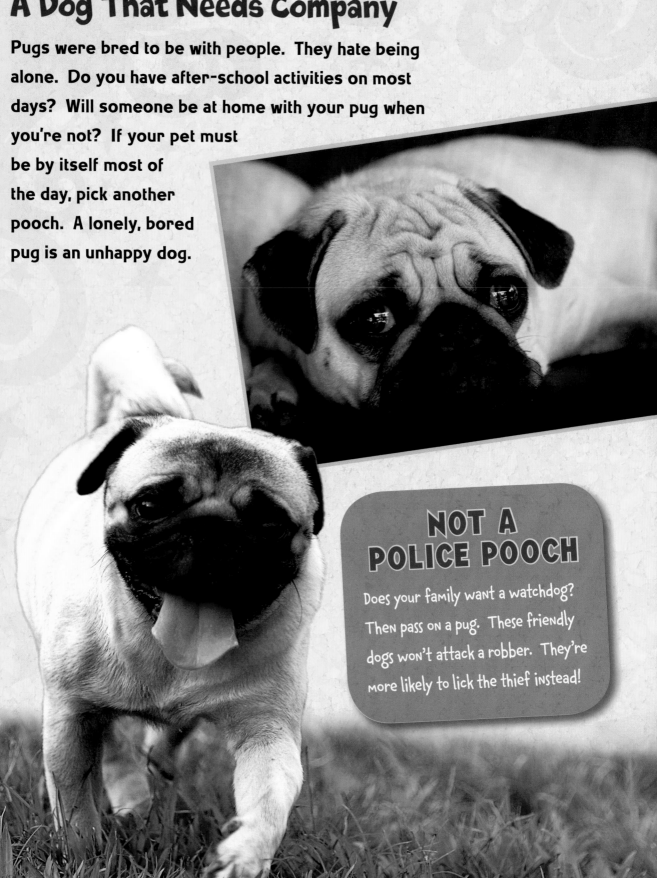

NOT A POLICE POOCH

Does your family want a watchdog? Then pass on a pug. These friendly dogs won't attack a robber. They're more likely to lick the thief instead!

The Right Place for a Pug

A pug can live happily in either the country or the city. It's small enough for apartment life too. But pugs can't live everywhere. They do not do well in places that are very hot or very cold.

Pugs have flat faces and short muzzles. Dogs like these can have trouble breathing in hot, humid places. And a pug's short fur doesn't keep it very warm in cold weather.

PUGS SNORE MORE

Pugs tend to snore a lot. Many flat-faced dogs do. Do you hope your new pug will sleep in your room? If so, snoring is something you may have to get used to.

This Small Dog Is Not Big on Exercise

Do you hope to go for daily jogs with your dog? Do you dream of long mountain hikes with your new pet? If so, don't get a pug. A short walk is enough exercise for this little dog. Going around the block two or three times a day would be perfect. Pugs like playing indoors with their toys too.

Is a pug the perfect pooch for you? If it is, get ready for lots of love and loads of laughs. A cute little clown of a dog is about to move in!

Pugs are playful dogs. They can make you laugh.

CHAPTER FOUR

WELCOMING YOUR PUG HOME

You've read all about the pug. You've decided that it's the dog for you. Now the big day is here. You're about to pick up your pug.

Make your new dog feel at home. Plan to spend the day with it. Buy the supplies you'll need before your pooch arrives.

Not sure what you'll need to welcome Fido to your family? This basic list is a great place to start:

• collar

• leash

• tags (for identification)

• dog food

• food and water bowls

• crates (one for when your pet travels by car and one for it to rest in at home)

• treats (to be used in training)

• toys

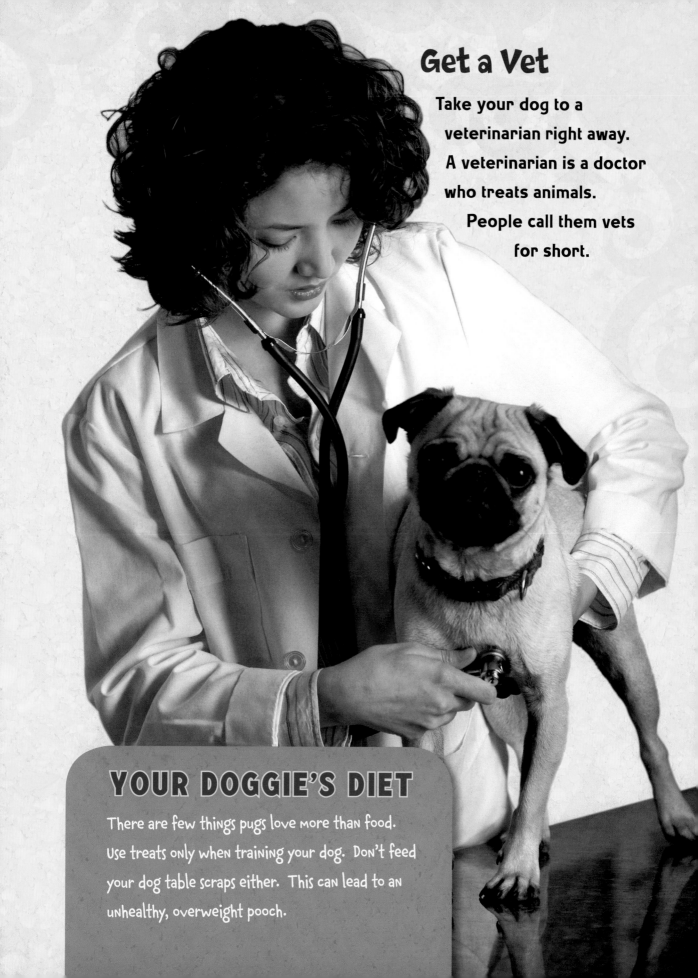

Get a Vet

Take your dog to a
veterinarian right away.
A veterinarian is a doctor
who treats animals.
People call them vets
for short.

YOUR DOGGIE'S DIET

There are few things pugs love more than food.
Use treats only when training your dog. Don't feed
your dog table scraps either. This can lead to an
unhealthy, overweight pooch.

Your vet will give your dog the shots it needs. Take your pooch back to the vet for regular checkups. Also take your pug to the vet if it gets sick.

Good Grooming

Brush your pug's coat a few times a week. This will remove any dead hair. Your pug's wrinkles need care as well. Use a soft baby wipe to gently clean the folds in your dog's skin.

You can use baby wipes to clean your pug's wrinkles.

You and Your Pug

All dogs need food and water. Pugs need
love almost as much. Your pug will want
to be at the center of your life.

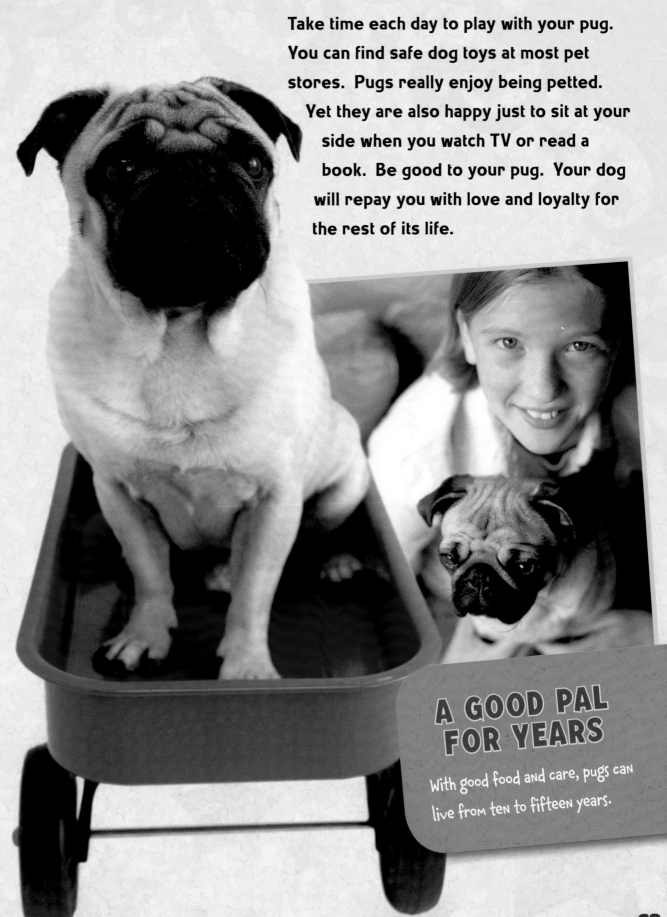

Take time each day to play with your pug. You can find safe dog toys at most pet stores. Pugs really enjoy being petted. Yet they are also happy just to sit at your side when you watch TV or read a book. Be good to your pug. Your dog will repay you with love and loyalty for the rest of its life.

A GOOD PAL FOR YEARS

With good food and care, pugs can live from ten to fifteen years.

GLOSSARY

American Kennel Club (AKC): an organization that groups dogs by breed. The AKC also defines the characteristics of different breeds.

breed: a particular type of dog. Dogs of the same breed have the same body shape and general features. *Breed* can also refer to producing puppies.

canine: a dog, or having to do with dogs

coat: a dog's fur

fawn: a shade of brown. Many pugs have fawn coats.

groom: to clean, brush, and trim a dog's coat

muzzle: a dog's nose, mouth, and jaws

shed: to lose fur

toy group: a group of different types of dogs that are all small in size

veterinarian: a doctor who treats animals. Veterinarians are called vets for short.

FOR MORE INFORMATION

Books

Brecke, Nicole, and Patricia M. Stockland. *Dogs You Can Draw*. Minneapolis: Millbrook Press, 2010. In this book especially for dog lovers, Brecke and Stockland show how to draw many different types of dogs.

Gray, Susan H. *Pugs*. Chanhassen, MN: Child's World, 2007. This fun selection tells all about pugs.

Houran, Lori Haskins. *Pug: What a Mug!* New York: Bearport, 2009. Read about some remarkable pugs—including Joseph, a pug who comforted a girl who had to be in the hospital on her birthday.

Landau, Elaine. *Shih Tzus Are the Best!* Minneapolis: Lerner Publications, 2011. If you love the pug, you may also like reading about the shih tzu—another adorable, flat-faced dog with roots in ancient China.

Landau, Elaine. *Your Pet Dog*. Rev. ed. New York: Children's Press, 2007. This book is a good guide for young people on choosing and caring for a dog.

Websites

American Kennel Club
http://www.akc.org
Visit this website to find a complete listing of AKC-registered dog breeds, including the pug. The site also features fun printable activities for kids.

ASPCA Animaland
http://www2.aspca.org/site/PageServer?pagename=kids_pc_home
Check out this page for helpful hints on caring for a dog and other pets.

Index

Photo Acknowledgments

The images in this book are used with the permission of: backgrounds © iStockphoto.com/Julie Fisher and © iStockphoto.com/Tomasz Adamczyk; © iStockphoto.com/Michael Balderas, p. 1; © Chris Lorenz/Dreamstime.com, p. 4; © Sarah M. Golonka/Getty Images, p. 5 (top); © ULTRA.F/ Digital Vision/Getty Images, p. 5 (bottom); © Andreas Gradin/Dreamstime.com, p. 6; © Eric Isselée/ Dreamstime.com, p. 7; © Bob Jacobson/CORBIS, p. 8; The Art Archive/Musée Cernuschi Paris/ Gianni Dagli Orti, p. 9; © Louis Michel van Loo/The Bridgeman Art Library/Getty Images, p. 10 (top); © Hulton Archive/Getty Images, p. 10 (bottom); © Bettmann/CORBIS, p. 11; © Chris Stein/The Image Bank/Getty Images, p. 12 (top); AP Photo/Ray Stubblebine, p. 12 (bottom); © Caro/Alamy, p. 13; © SuperStock, Inc./SuperStock, p. 14 (left); © GK Hart/Vikki Hart/Photodisc/Getty Images, p. 14 (center); © iStockphoto.com/Eric Isselée, p. 14 (right); © Andrey Medvedev/Dreamstime.com, p. 15 (top left); © Jesse Kunerth/Dreamstime.com, p. 15 (top right); © Willeecole/Dreamstime.com, p. 15 (bottom); © Maria Sweeney/Taxi/Getty Images, p. 16; © Lucy Snowe/SuperStock, p. 17; © Reggie Casagrande/Digital Vision/Getty Images, p. 18 (top); © Melvinlee/Dreamstime.com, p. 18 (bottom); © Graca Victoria/Dreamstime.com, p. 19 (top); © Dominik Eckelt/Photographer's Choice/ Getty Images, p. 19 (bottom); © Chris Jackson/Getty Images, p. 20; © Juniors Bildarchiv/Alamy, pp. 21, 24; © Bstefanov/Dreamstime.com, pp. 22–23; © Tanya Constantine/Photodisc/Getty Images, p. 23; © April Turner/Dreamstime.com, p. 24 (top inset); © Tammy Mcallister/Dreamstime.com, p. 24 (bottom inset); © Ariel Skelley/CORBIS, p. 25; © LWA-Dann Tardif/CORBIS, p. 26; © John Steel/Dreamstime.com, p. 27 (top); © Martin Green/Dreamstime.com, p. 27 (center); © Indeed/ Stockbyte/Getty Images, p. 27 (bottom); © Noel Hendrickson/CORBIS, p. 28; © Koki Iino/Getty Images, p. 29 (left); © Ryan McVay/Digital Vision/Getty Images, p. 29 (right).

Front cover: © iStockphoto.com/Andrew Johnson.
Back cover: © Hanhanpeggy/Dreamstime.com.